Happy bi[...]
2/86   & many more
Love,
Dad &
Russell

ALASKA
SOURDOUGH

RUTH ALLMAN

ALASKA NORTHWEST PUBLISHING COMPANY
Anchorage, Alaska

Copyright © 1976 by Ruth Allman.
All rights reserved. No part of this book may
be reproduced or transmitted in any form
or by any means, electromc or mechanical,
including photocopying, recording or by any
information storage and retrieval system without
written permission of Alaska Northwest
Publishing Company.

First printing: 1976
Seventh printing: 1983

Library of Congress cataloging in publication data:
Allman, Ruth, 1905-
  Alaska sourdough.
  1. Cookery (Sourdough) I. Title.
TX770.A44   641.6'3'11   76-13604
ISBN 0-88240-085-1

Alaska Northwest Publishing Company
Box 4-EEE, Anchorage, Alaska 99509
Printed in U.S.A.

Dedicated
to
Alaskan—Yukon Sourdoughs

"Who mined at Circle and Klondike creeks.
Who camped at Nome, 'neath Anvil's peaks
Who founded Fairbanks, opened its mines,
And prospected where the Iditarod twines;

Who built its town, its roads and trails,
Who planned its railroads, and laid the rails;
Who g'uide in council, in creating homes,
And in laying a State's foundation stones."

...Judge James Wickersham
1857 - 1939

An Eskimo's
Interpretation of
"Fast Day."

"EAT LESS MORE
GET SAVED FASTER."

Contents

Ruth and Sourdough

I was raised by Judge and Mrs. Wickersham, Alaska pioneers of the 1900 vintage. I had heard about and had experienced much of the frontier life, but only a limited amount of really roughing it.

When I married Jack Allman, our first home was miles from the nearest neighbor or grocery store. We were truly on our own.

So now, Sourdough was to become our main source of food — and I did not know how to use it!

2

Jack was an expert and a patient teacher. He had many years of experiences using Sourdough, and was a great admirer of its qualities. He had been dependent on it for food in the mining camps, and on the trail. It had become a way of life with him.

The first cabin we had, Jack built a shelf in back of the Yukon-stove pipe for the Sourdough Pot! Actually the shelf rated "top priority," as he built it before he took time to set up the bed or put up the furniture. He wanted to be certain the Sourdough would be kept warm and continue bubbling — ready to keep us in food.

At that time no cook books were available with Sourdough recipes. Everyone had his own recipe. No one considered a cook book.

Sourdough was known as the best food for energy. Mix a rich thick potato water with flour, and a spoonful or two of sugar, and you have the beginnings of a Sourdough Pot. Keep it in a warm place and it will begin to ferment. A "wild yeast" develops. The Sourdough is beginning to work, emitting a profusion of small effervescent bubbles. Thus you have created the "Bubbling Sourdough." Truly this is a miracle worker. Transforming what was apparently a starch food into a protein dynamo!

There are some modern cooks who say, "Fold stiffly beaten egg whites into the Sourdough batter to make it light and fluffy."

Pioneer Alaskans did not have the luxury of fresh eggs. If anyone had ever experienced "Chinese Eggs" or "Cold Storage Eggs", the strong taste would perish the thought of adding them to Sourdough!

Instead, the pioneer would just add a teaspoonful of good old "Arm and Hammer" baking soda to the batch of Sourdough Starter. As it is folded in, instantly a chemical action takes place. Remember the _sour_ dough has acid qualities, and soda is a spontaneous neutralizer and sweetener.

As you fold the soda in, the batter starts to raise, filling the bowl with fluffy Sourdough. You can feel the change as you are spooning the batter over and over. There is a hollow tone developing, deeper and deeper as the Sourdough becomes filled with millions of tiny air bubbles.

Make certain everything is ready — the iron or griddle hot, so the Sourdough can be cooked while the air is still working in the batter. Results: You have "50% baked hot air" and light Sourdoughs that melt in your mouth.

Delay in hitting the iron until after the Sourdough stops raising and you will have a flat batter. Bake while air is in the Sourdough for buoyant delicious mouth-watering Sourdoughs!

6

The analysis of laboratory tests have shown Sourdough contains the greatest amount of protein for its weight and size of any comparable food.

There are reports that food scientists for the "Moon Mission" had considered Sourdough wafers for the space flights because of the high protein content. Crumbs became a problem — Sourdough was not ready for Space, yet!

Many modern advocates of Sourdough claim milk should be added to the Starter instead of using water, believing it makes a richer batter for Sourdough hotcakes or Sourdough biscuits. Truly these should be considered sour milk hotcakes or sour milk biscuits. Yes, they too are delicious, but

they should not be confused with
the distinctive _taste_ of _pure_ Sourdough.

Sourdough mellows with age.
If milk is used in lieu of water in the
Starter, it wouldn't take long for it
to become rancid with an over-powering
pungent odor — compared to the
rich yeast _smell_ of _pure_ Sourdough.

Milk was extremely difficult to get
and seldom available on the trail,
and definitely not a part of the
original pioneer Sourdough cooking
of Sourdough hotcakes, biscuits or
other food stuffs.

Sourdoughs never need to have the strong sour taste — only a fresh yeasty flavor. Do not add sugar to sweeten. Remember <u>Soda</u> <u>Sweetens</u>.

Sugar is very important, as it will give the golden brown color to your Sourdoughs. Use only a spoonful or two. <u>Too much</u> <u>sugar</u> will toughen - it gives a leathery quality.

It does take time for the Sourdough "wild yeast" to work. Some modern cooks get impatient and use a Yeastcake or a spoonful of baking powder. True, this does speed up the baking time. But only use it as a <u>crutch</u>. Do not

destroy the real savor of the pure
Sourdough with these substitutes.

I have been prompted to write this
book regarding my experiences, as well
as to record early legends, stories and
recipes of pioneer Alaskans. I am
also including recipes that I have
developed myself for Sourdough.
Pioneer printing facilities were very
limited. Many early Alaskan papers were
hand written. Jack used birch bark
in lieu of writing paper while on the
trail. So, I decided to hand letter and
illustrate this book with rough pen-
sketches — just for You.
Remember the Sourdough Greeting:
"The Latch String is out, and the
    Sourdough Pot is a-bubbling!"

Ruth

Saga of

ALASKA

Sourdough

Saga of Sourdough

Sourdough: A Canadian or an Alaskan prospector...so called from the habit of carrying Sourdough, a fermented dough, used as a leaven in making bread.

(Webster's Collegiate Dictionary - 5th edition)

A good enough definition as far as it goes. However, it fails to mention or even give a

W.   E.

S.

hint at the important place this prerequisite to all good breadstuffs holds in the self prepared menus of the men of the High North.

During our pioneer days in Alaska, we have introduced many Cheechakos (newcomers) to the archetypal Sourdough hotcake. And from this introduction have received nods of approval in consequence...

Only a short time ago a lady house guest said, "Ruth, these Sourdough hotcakes are heavenly!"

It was a pretty way of voicing her approval, but it was also an unconscious plagiarism.

Sourdough was likened unto heaven in the very first English translation of the Bible. In 1382 John Wycliff, in good old Chaucer English, translated as follows: Matthew XIII : 33.

"An other parable Jhesus spac to hem. The Kyngdom of hevenes is like soure dowz, the whiche taken, a womman hidde in three mesuris of meel, til it were all sowrdowid."*

Matthew 13 : 33

Rightfully, Sourdough has been associated with frontiers men in the minds of the last two generations. It has been the man of the hills, the woods, and far places who has earned

*The Century Dictionary and Cyclopedia, Vol. VII, page 5785. Copyright, 1889, 1895, 1897, by The Century Co.

Sour dough, leaven; a fermented mass of dough left from a previous mixing, and used as a ferment to raise a fresh batch of dough. [Obsolete or prov. Eng.]

An other parable Jhesus spac to hem, The kyngdam of heuenes is lic to soure dowz, the whiche taken, a womman hidde in three mesuris of meele, til it were al sowrdowid.
Wyclif, Mat. xiii. 33.

the right to proudly wear its name as his Sobriquet : "Sourdough"!

Sourdough is an international pioneer food. Alaska has made it more significant than any other section — the last frontier. California pioneers called it "Sourdough", but the cattle country called it "Chuck Wagon Bread". South Dakota pioneers referred to their bread as "Cellar Biscuits or Bread" as they always kept their Sourdough in the cellar. In Philadelphia the pioneer could buy a cup of "Yeast Dough" for one penny. Kentucky called it "Spook yeast" because so airy and fluffy — and baked "Spook Bread".
In Germany you have "Sauerteig" — a counterpart of our Sourdough. In Africa they have a wild yeast called "Möst"!

15

Yeast was extremely difficult for the pioneer cook to get during the early days in Alaska. And frequently when they were able to get it, the yeast would be "dead", after being exposed to extreme conditions of time and cold. Poor yeast would cause baking failures. This was not only a disappointment for the cook, it was a serious waste of supplies.

Sourdough was the solution for the baking problem, as it was a perpetual source of yeast, and always available. Furthermore, the camp cook knew it was dependable, and had no fear of a baking failure because of "dead" yeast.

The famed Klondike
Gold Rush of '98, not only
started one of the greatest
stampedes, it firmly
established Sourdough as the
most popular and practical food
for the pioneer, and prospector.

Food was scarce. You rated
as a millionaire if you had plenty
of grub, even tho not a dime in
your jeans. Provisions were
more valuable than gold. One
had to eat!

"If you are going to the Klondike
I'll tell you what to do,
Better take a ton of grub —
Or better yet — take Two!"

The Canadian Mounted Police
refused to let any of the goldseekers
over the boundary at Chilkoot Pass
without a year's supply of provisions,

Many a stampeder had to "neck" his
own sled—pulling it himself—as he
did not have the price of a dog.

So, it was of utmost importance to
get the "mostest from the leastest"
when making out his grub list. Often
a year's supply of grub would be
stored in a food cache; a log cabin
built high off the ground to keep
the provisions safe from marauding
wild animals.

Soon they discovered a
50-pound sack of potatoes

would easily freeze. A 50-pound
sack of flour — and a Sourdough
Pot — would guarantee more
satisfactory meals than canned
food many times its weight.

Professional packers
charged $1.00 per pound for
every item carried. This
quickly mounted to a terrific
item. The pioneer was anxious
to have supplies that lasted.

In 1899 Dr. and Mrs. W.T. Miles
started the first drug store in Nome.
They considered themselves lucky
to have brought two-tons of
provisions with them when they
saw the prices in that wind swept

town on the Bering Sea. Butter sold for $5.00 a pound; condensed milk $50.00 per case; coal $125.00 per ton; even a pail of water cost 50 cents.

Food demanded respect. Circle City in 1900 was a booming tent city of 10,000 gold seekers. A man was given a death sentence for stealing a pound can of butter from a food cache. Stealing food was more serious than murder.

Many legends have been handed down from the pioneer era of Alaska. Somehow, word got around that baking powder, like salt peter, was an anaphrodisiac. The he-man of the North was justly proud of his virility, as attested by the size of some of Alaska's half-breed families.

He took no chances of his libido being impaired. The old-time Alaskan would not include baking powder biscuits in his regular diet. Thus, was born the fame and popularity of Sourdough.

That statement about baking powder was given credence was very clearly shown during the Chisana Stampede, (the last big gold stampede in Alaska - 1913). About one hundred prospectors camped on one spot of the upper reaches of the Tanana River. The only woman in camp was one of the sisterhood whose charms were for sale wherever a mining camp sprung up.

Maud's tent stood on the river bank, a short way down stream from the main camp. She didn't have one customer during the month she was there. No gold had been mined and everyone had sunk his last dollar into tools, equipment, and a winter's grub supply. The whole crowd would not have assayed a twenty dollar piece.

One of the stampeders became disheartened and declared his intention of riding the river back to Fairbanks, a distance of four or five hundred miles. Maud, by this time thoroughly disgusted with her business venture, decided to return to Fairbanks with him.

The poling boat was soon loaded with their gear, and as it shoved off into the current Maud looked up at the bunch of fellows lining the bank.

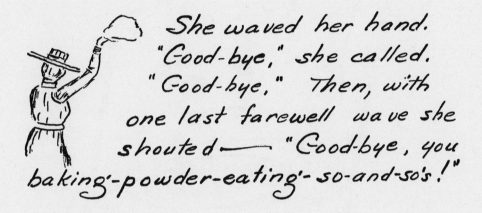 She waved her hand. "Good-bye," she called. "Good-bye," Then, with one last farewell wave she shouted —— "Good-bye, you baking-powder-eating-so-and-so's!"

There are still a number of the fellows around who stood on the bank that day and were to receive Maud's classic adieu. The story is usually repeated whenever the merits of Sourdough are discussed.

Sourdough Pot

Alaska's Flag
"Eight stars of gold
On a field of blue..."

Then . . .

Here's to the man on the trail . . .

May his dogs keep their legs . . .

May his grub hold out . . . and

May his matches never miss fire.

         . . . Jack London

Sourdough Pot

A perfect duo. The Sourdough and his Sourdough Pot. They have become an important part of Alaska and the historic legends of the North.

Today Sourdough is as modern as tomorrow; is unusually active, and has not been forgotten with yesteryear.

Many a sportsman will select his guide, not because of his proficiency in knowing the trails, but rather one that can be relied on to tote along a Sourdough Pot, of ancient vintage. This will insure the camp a good Sourdough feed during the expedition.

A real Alaskan Sourdough would as soon spend a year in the hills without his rifle, as to tough it through without his bubbling Sourdough Pot.

It is the "prime pelt" in the larder of the trapper; the "gold bearing vein" in the food cache of the hardrock miner; It is all important to the one who lives all alone on some nameless creek, and is utterly dependent on himself for all his food.

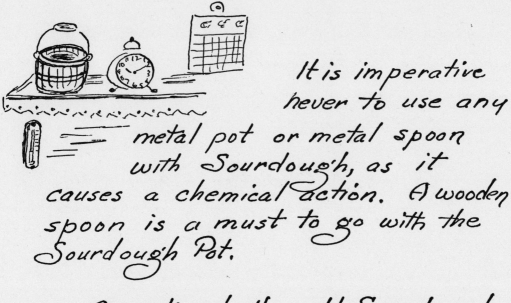

It is imperative never to use any metal pot or metal spoon with Sourdough, as it causes a chemical action. A wooden spoon is a must to go with the Sourdough Pot.

According to the old Sourdough himself, the best container is a small wooden pail that holds a gallon or more. It is less subject to sudden changes in temperature to below-zero weather.

In the old log cabin, the prospector would have the Sourdough Pot swinging from the drying rack over the little sheet iron Yukon stove. Or it would be sitting on a special shelf in back of the stove pipe.

28

Sourdough works best when the room temperature is between 65° and 77°.

There is a serious problem when the thermometer skids down to -50°. Many a winter traveller has wrapped his Sourdough Pot in a canvas tarp and taken it to bed to keep it from freezing — to make certain he would have his Sourdough for food tomorrow.

While mushing on the trail with the temperature flirting below zero, Jack would put some Sourdough in an old Prince Albert tobacco can. This he tucked inside the pocket of his wool shirt to make certain it would not freeze.

It takes very little Sourdough to start the old Sourdough Pot a-bubbling again.

The old battery jars (from the relay station of the first and the temporary overland telegraph line from salt water to the Yukon River) have furnished many an old timer with an ideal Sourdough Pot. Many are still in use.

Glass jars were not too popular during the early days. There was such a risk of breakage when travelling over rough trails by dogteam.

Today's transportation presents a different problem for the Sourdough Pot. Plane - train - or auto travel is a far cry from mushing on the trail fifty years ago. Caution should be exercised to keep the Sourdough cool — refrigeration if possible - while Travelling. Heat and pressure cause Sourdough'n to expand.

A sportsman packed his Sourdough Pot, along with his fishing gear, in the trunk of his car.

When he got to rolling down the road toward a real vacation — the Sourdough was rolling too. Heat, plus the motion of the car, created a real Mount Vesuvius in the back end of the auto. Sourdough oozed out and over everywhere — and into the wide open spaces. What a mess! But the accident could have been prevented by a bit of early planning. A thermo container would have kept the Starter from getting heated and causing expansion.

A similar experience happened to an old Sourdough flying to the States for the winter, taking a Starter with him. He never thought to ask to have it put in the cooler during the flight.

Heat, plus motion, plus altitude caused a strain on that container as those Sourdough enzymes began working overtime. The area was a mess when the Sourdough exploded.. Oozing luscious Sourdough over all.

The old prospector had a sure way of travelling with his Sourdough. He buried his Sourdough in the top of his sack of flour — warm and safe.

When he arrived at camp, many times he only added flour and water to make the right quantity and consistency, without taking Sourdough from the flour sack. Saved a dish when no dish was available.

1903. Sourdough was an important food of the FIRST attempt to climb Mt. McKinley, the expedition organized by Alaska's pioneer Judge James Wickersham.

Two mules were used to pack supplies. A 300 pound sack of flour, an important item for Sourdough, was the basic food of man as well as the mules. Animals crave the wild yeast of the Sourdough.

No Sourdough Pot! They carried the Starter in top of the flour.

To make Sourdoughs, they poured the glacial water - heavy with silt - and made the dough right in the flour sack. Then rolled The Sourdough on the end of a stick and baked in front of an open fire.

The Judge would say, "Young Lady, if you are really hungry - even sand will fill your craw!"

Early day travellers experienced many emergencies on the trail in Alaska. It might be capsizing of the river boat or canoe while riding the rapids. Or falling off the dog sled with you and all provisions going down the mountain side. All can be disastrous — to you and the Sourdough Pot.

Mary Lee Davis, in her book "Uncle Sam's Attic," tells how an old prospector, having lost his pack mule because of a snowslide, had rolled down over the snow barrier and quickly scraped into his empty tobacco tin some of the Sourdough that spilled from his broken Sourdough Pot — and smeared it over his dead beast's nose!

To such extremes the Alaskan
pioneer Sourdough will go
to preserve and retain his
beloved Sourdough Pot - - -
his staff of life!

Sourdough Starter

Sourdough Starter

Sourdough Starter is perfectly described by the name: simply that which starts the Sourdough Pot bubbling, and always some left as a starter for the next batch. A perpetual supply of Sourdough with a minimum amount of care.

It is most versatile. Best known as a leaven for Sourdough Hots. Worked into a stiff dough, it becomes a bread of real substance — whether baked in the oven of a temperamental Yukon stove, or on a hot rock heaped around with red glowing birch coals — or a kitchen oven with controlled heat.

Basicaly Sourdough Starter was used as a supply of food — bread, hotcakes cookies, cakes, yes, even waffles if the pioneer was lucky enough to have the old black iron for waffles. Generally it was too heavy for the prospector to carry.

Sourdough Starter also came in handy tanning hides. Lay the skin flat on a board with fur side down. Then rub Sourdough into the skin until soft and dry.

Many a prospector made a "Plaster" using Sourdough when he had a "stitch in his back" — or lumbago.

Sourdough came in handy as a paste pot when papering the cabin with a news paper — if lucky enough to have one. Or to seal a letter in lieu of glue.

How to Start a Sourdough Starter

Simplest method:

Obtain a cup of Starter from an active working Sourdough Pot. Even a "smidgen of a cup" of Starter will get the busy little enzymes working to build up a bubbling Sourdough Pot.

Dump Starter in a jar or crock to be used as the Sourdough Pot. Add: (approximate proportions)

2 cups water — rich potato water
2 cups flour
2 tbsp. sugar

Salt is omitted for it retards the action.

Sugar used to speed up action — not to sweeten — and to brown the Sourdoughs.

Now, just in case there is no Sourdough Starter available — just start your own. It's fun! It's easy!

Sourdough Starter

Dump into the Sourdough Pot

2 cups thick potato water
2 tbsp. sugar
2 cups flour (more or less)
½ tsp. yeast (optional) *

Boil potatoes with jackets on until they fall to pieces. Lift skins out; mash potatoes making a puree. Cool. Add more water to make sufficient liquid, if necessary. Richer the potato water, richer the Starter. Put all ingredients in Pot. Beat until smooth creamy batter. Cover. Set aside in warm place to start fermentation. *Use yeast only to speed action.

Grated Potato Starter

2 raw potatoes
grated in bottom of the
Sourdough Pot.
1 Yeast cake, diluted in
2 cups warm water
2 tbsp. sugar
Flour enough to make a
smooth, creamy batter.

Beat well. Get all lumps out
at this time so it is not necessary
to remove any flour lumps later
when ready to use the Starter.

Cover. Place Sourdough
Pot on the shelf in a warm spot,
free from draughts.

This Starter takes longer to start
working, but in a week it will be bubbling:

How Long?

Just how long
does it take the Sourdough Starter
to become "ripe" — in prime working condition?

Exponents differ.

3-Day-Starter: Sourdough Starter
can be used now, providing those little
enzymes have started working. But
it is better to wait a few more days.
Toss in extra fuel for the Sourdough
to work on — a spoonful of sugar
along with a couple spoonsful of flour.
Add water if batter too thick. Mix well.
Cover. Put in warm spot to work more.

1-Week-Starter: Starter is now
effervescing with a million bubbles.
Looks like sour cream — smells like sour cream,
but is rich luscious Sourdough.

<u>2-Week-Starter</u>: Disciples of Sourdough claim that waiting this extra time gives extra flavor, which is not to be compared with any other batter.

<u>3-Week-Starter</u>: The Sourdough Pot is now bubbling like the old witch's cauldron.

<u>1-Month-Starter</u>: Sourdough is now a rich creamy batter that is honey combed with bubbles.

<u>1-Year-Starter</u>:   Oldtimer's claim a year must elapse before the Sourdough matures and offers the distinctive taste appeal nothing else can imitate —— Sourdough!

43

With a wooden spoon, whip the Starter smooth. There is nothing worse than to find lumps of flour in your Sourdough.

Use a wooden spoon, as a metal spoon causes the little enzymes to work overtime on the metal.

If batter seems stiff and heavy, add more water — enough to make a rich, thick creamy sponge. It is best to have the batter thicker as it will thin down while working over night.

If the Starter is very thin, throw in extra flour to make a smooth creamy batter.

Cover. Let the Starter "work" in a warm place, free from draughts.

44

The Alaska natives were not familiar with the Sourdough Pot until introduced to it by the white man. It is amazing how suddenly they caught on— and how they made a potent brew.

Sourdough beer is simple to make but disagreeable to drink. But, if consumed in quantity, will produce any desired degree of intoxication.

All one needs is a barrel, flour, and some water. Into this pour some Sourdough and Dame Nature takes its course from there. A little sugar will speed up matters, but even without it, those smelly little ascomycetes will soon acquaint your neighbors with the fact you have brew in the making.

After the solids have sunk to the bottom all that remains is for the imbibers to gather around with tin cups, and dip deep into the malodorous liquid. Beewack is never bottled. Only a fool would carry a live bomb.

Care should be exercised, however, when one nears the bottom of the barrel. Not many years ago an Aleut from down Dutch Harbor way slipped while dipping deep and drowned in his own barrel. His drinking companions were all too befuddled to drag him out.

"Long Sugar" - known as Molasses today, was used by the early day pioneer and native . Using an old rifle barrel and a trade pot, they created a still. Resultant spirits were known by the Thlinget word - "Hooch-m-noo" - from which we get the term "Hootch."

Do not let Sourdough freeze . Remember the Sourdough Starter is a wild yeast composed of busy little enzymes that are ambitious and great workers. They give up mighty fast when temperature gets down to freezing.

Age improves and mellows the taste appeal of Sourdough.

Today you can hear an Alaskan, say with pride that their "Sourdough is forty years old." or perhaps that they can "trace their Starter to the days when Fairbanks was a mining camp."

Descendants of the Mayflower have nothing on the proud lineage of many a Sourdough Starter.

Recently a representative of a large New York department store came to Alaska to obtain a Starter "of early vintage", as they wished to feature Sourdough bakery goods in their tea room.

When given a scant cupful in a quart container, an amazed look followed. "But we need enough to serve 500 Sourdoughs a day!"

Very small amount of Sourdough Starter can be increased — simply by adding flour and water, with a dash of sugar,

and letting it "work" in a warm place.

Shortly after the New Yorkers returned home, word was received: "Have 2 tubs of bubbling Sourdough Starter ready to use."

WARNING

Take precautions when carrying or storing Sourdough Starter.

Allow plenty of room for expansion as Sourdough when "working" can more than double content.

Keep Sourdough at constant room temperature. Extreme cold will cause the Sourdough "to go flat". Sudden heat will cause excessive expansion.

Sourdough makes Headlines

Fairbanks (A.P.)... A joking remark about a Sourdough Starter setting off a bomb scare, turned out delaying a P.A.A flight for 2 hours.

A passenger, boarding the plane with a jar of Sourdough Starter. Jokingly remarked, "..hope it wouldn't blow up!" The stewardess overheard and reported to the pilot of the scare.

Immediately orders were given for all passengers to deplane and all personal baggage was checked.

International Airport security officers, state police and F.B.I. officials participated in the search and discovered a quart jar of luscious bubbling Sourdough!

Sealed in a jar, without room for expansion, it could have exploded. Heat and motion of the plane would make the Sourdough work overtime.

Never keep Sourdough in a tight container.

50

Sourdough Hotcakes

Sourdough Hotcakes

*"For those who know their Hotcakes best,
It's Sourdoughs — two to one!"*

The real blue ribbon product
of the Sourdough Pot, of course,
is the tasty hotcake.

Sourdough hotcakes have nothing
in common with other breeds, except
shape and color. The taste is distinctive enough to demand all

your attention, even when swimming in syrup or smeared with jam, jelly or honey.

This robust and hairy-chested relative of the crepe suzette, is strictly an individual and stands alone. It is not to be confused in any manner with the common flap-jack, the flannel cake, or the many garden varieties of the griddle cake.

Sourdough hotcakes, the main breakfast dish of the prospector, miner, and the old time Alaskan.

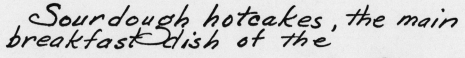

Essentially a break-fast dish, Sourdough

hot cakes can be pressed into service for any meal. You will never go hungry as long as you have a Sourdough Pot working and a sack of flour to keep it going. There are many flour "stretchers" such as Oatmeal, Buckwheat, etc. But these change the taste, and you cannot get the "pure Sourdough" back until you start one again. One time, in desperation, we used the cattail down as a flour-stretcher, making saffron colored Sourdoughs — I don't recommend it!

Our two registered Siamese cats, Tu Yung Tu and No Yen Tu, as well as Billy, the dog refused to eat their prepared food when they smelled Sourdoughs cooking. They'd beg until I would throw one down. hot from the griddle, hoping to burn their noses. But they

Billy

Tu Yung Tu   No Yen Tu

would pick up the Sourdough, shake it, and down it in one gulp—and beg for more. They seemed to crave the wild yeast in Sourdough.

What did they feed the pack horse when they had no hay? Sourdoughs! When Jack and his partner crossed the Scolai Glacier, they fed their famished horse Sourdough hotcakes. So eager was the horse to get the hotcakes, Jack nearly lost a finger in the process.

Jack was known as the Spirited Kid, and had sled dogs known as the Spirited Team: Tom and Jerry, Rum, Gin, Brandy, Whiskey and Hootch. He finally got a lead dog from old Chief Issac. This became "Chaser", for where there were so may "Spirits", one had to have a chaser! While on the trail he fed the dogs dried fish and Sourdoughs.

I have yet to meet a person who didn't like a well turned out mess of Sourdough hot cakes.

There are some Cheechakos who evince an enthusiam that is akin to a mania. Hardly to a degree, though, of the maiden lady, who upon insistence of her family, visited a psychiatrist. In answer to his queries, she said that her folks insisted she was crazy because of her fondness for good hotcakes.

"Why, that's nothing to be concerned about," said the young psychiatrist. "I am extremely fond of good hotcakes myself!"

56

"You are?" she exclaimed. "Oh, that is wonderful. You must come up and visit me at my home. I have trunks and trunks of them!"

Many a fanciful tale has been spun around the campfire concerning the merits of Sourdough. Some of the tales are fantastic, but they are "told" always with genuine enthusiasm and fact.

Justice William O. Douglas, of the United States Supreme Court, is an outstanding fishing enthusiast and a great advocate of Sourdough. He always carries a Sourdough pot with him on his fishing trips.

As a matter of fact, Justice Douglas insists that his Sourdough hotcakes and Sourdough biscuits are so "lacking with avoirdupois that very frequently they would be carried away by mosquitoes and gnats."

To remedy this dilemma he would "every so often mix in some blueberries or raisins, so that only the strongest and biggest insects could soar away with them!"

Basic Recipe
Sourdough Hotcakes

2 cups Sourdough Starter
2 tbsp. sugar
4 tbsp. oil
1 egg
1/2 tsp. salt
1 scant tsp. soda ; full teaspoon
        if Starter is real sour.

Into the Sourdough, dump sugar, egg and oil. Mix well. Add soda the last thing, when ready for batter to hit the griddle. Dilute soda in 1 tbsp. of warm water. Fold gently into Sourdough. Do not beat. Notice deep hollow tone as Sourdough fills with bubbles and doubles bulk. Bake on hot griddle to seal brown. Serve on hot plates.

Alaska
Blueberry
Sourdoughs

To Basic Sourdough Recipe
Add: 1 cup blueberries dusted with
      2 tbsp. sugar
Let stand a few minutes; fold gently
into the batter just before adding
the soda.

or

Spoon the batter on the hot griddle
Sprinkle fresh blueberries over the
top of the hotcakes.

Bake until berries are cooked through.
Turn; Serve on hot plates with
maple sugar and sausages.

Corned Beef Sourdoughs

To basic recipe add
    1 cup (or can) Corned beef
        mashed into small pieces.
    1 tsp. Worcestershire sauce
Mix meat in batter well before
    adding the soda.
Bake slowly until golden brown.

Serve with scrambled egg or
    fried sauer kraut
To reheat: brush each Sourdough
    with butter. Place on tray and
    pop into the oven to heat thru.
Wonderful for camp menu. Use
    wild game meat for a wonderful
    substitute: venison, moose, caribou!

Sourdough
Cheese
Hotcakes

Use basic Sourdough recipe.
Before adding the soda, stir in:
    ½ cup tangy grated cheese
    1 tbsp. Worcestershire sauce
    dash of Tabasco (optional)
Fold in 1 tsp. soda dissolved in
1 tbsp. water just before baking
dollar-sized Sourdoughs.

Wonderful accompaniment
served with boiled fish and lemon
butter.

Note: Sourdough Cheese Appetizers
Spread anchovy butter on tiny
hotcakes — or cut small — serve hot.

Sourdough Jim's
Clam - Buckwheat Hots

Night before fix a "buckwheat starter." Pour 2 cups Sourdough in a bowl. Use clam nectar for liquid, (1 cup) Add buckwheat flour (1 cup) along with white flour (1 cup). Keep bowl in a warm place to "work" over night.

Morning: To 2 cups Buckwheat Starter add: 1 egg
  4 tbsp oil
  2 tbsp. sugar
  ½ cup — 1 cup minced clams.
Add 1 tsp. soda diluted in warm water when griddle is ready to bake.
Serve with crisp bacon.
Warning: do not add Buckwheat to the main Sourdough Pot. Always take out to make special Buckwheat Sourdough.

Sourdough Clam Hots

Mix basic Sourdough recipe.
Before adding soda — stir in —
3/4 cup clams — well drained,
     coarsely chopped.
1 tbsp. grated onion
1 tsp. chopped parsley
1/2 tsp. pepper

Mix clams into batter. When skillet is
hot, fold in 1 tsp. soda diluted in warm
water. Stir gently. Do not beat.
When batter fluffs, doubling in its
bulk, dip to skillet to bake Sourdoughs.
    Serve hot with sauce:
    1 cup catsup
    3 tbsp. lemon juice
Garnish with green pepper
strips, parsley and wedges
of lemon.

Apple Sauce Sourdoughs

Basic recipe for Sourdoughs.
Applesauce — well seasoned
with cinnamon and nutmeg.

On hot, well greased skillet drop
Sourdough making small pancakes.
Dip a small teaspoonful sauce
in center of each cake.
Add a few drops of Sourdough
batter, covering the applesauce.
Bake until bubbly.
Turn carefully, cooking well on
the other side.
Serve hot on warmed plates.
Dust Sourdoughs with powdered
sugar.

Sourdough Pineapple Hotcakes

Using basic recipe add dash of powdered cloves to the batter.
Drain well 2-3 slices pineapple until dry. Snip in thin slivers. add to batter before soda is added. When griddle is hot, add soda diluted in water. Fold in. Do not beat after soda is added. Bake to golden brown.

Lemon - Coconut Sourdoughs

Add to basic recipe:
   1 tbsp. grated lemon rind
   1/3 cup grated coconut
Bake dollar size hotcakes,
Serve with warm butter - maplesugar
or Rosehip syrup

Strawberry Stack
o' Sourdoughs

Using basic Sourdough recipe
bake stack of large thin Sourdoughs.
Place on piping hot oven plate
that has been well buttered.
As each Sourdough is baked, spread
with melted butter and brown sugar,
adding layer on layer.
Cover stack with swirls of meringue.

2 egg whites beaten stiff and dry.
1/2 cup powdered sugar
1/4 tsp. lemon juice

Brown under broiler to delicate brown.
Serve piping hot with Strawberries —
fresh or frozen — that have just been
brought to a boil.
Cut in wedges. Garnish with fresh
Strawberries. Serve on warm plates.

Sourdough Apple Hots

To Basic Sourdough
    Hotcake Recipe, add:
1 cup finely diced apples
    dusted generously with
2 tbsp. brown sugar and
½ tsp. cinnamon
    dash nutmeg
Bake dollar-size hotcakes on hot
griddle . Serve with brown sugar
melted in butter.

. . . . . or try . . . . .
Apple Ring Sourdoughs

Place a very thin slice of apple ring on
top of each Sourdough hotcake, just
the size of the apple ring. Bake brown.
  Serve with home made sausage.
  Wonderful to complement a pork roast.

Russian America Blintz

To basic Sourdough recipe, add extra egg. This will make batter very thin, as you want paper thin 7-inch Sourdough hotcakes. Bake only one side until blistered with bubbles.

Blintz Filling:

2 cups Cottage Cheese (dry)

1 egg yolk

1 tbsp. sugar

2 tsp. melted butter

2 tsp. grated orange rind

¼ tsp. cinnamon

salt to taste.

Place a spoonful of filling in center of each Sourdough — on the baked side.

Fold over all four sides envelope fashion. Seal with dab of Sourdough. Bake on the griddle until brown on both sides.

Serve with sour cream ---or fruit--

SITKA RUSSIAN Church

Sourdough Surprises

Blossom out with sweet surprises.

Variety is the spice of life and
surprises add the zest. With very
little effort and plenty of imagination,
simple Sourdough with its flavor
packed nutrition can be tops in
eye appeal as well as taste appeal.

Children love surprises! Treat
them to festive Sourdoughs.
They are fun to make. Wonderful
to serve for children's luncheon or a
tea party. A delight to see disappear
with eager appetites.

Orange
Sourdough Hots

Mix basic Sourdough recipe.
Before adding soda, mix in grated rind of one orange.   Add soda diluted in warm water when ready to bake Sourdoughs.

Sourdough Orange Cones

Bake 5-inch Sourdough Orange hots. Gently roll hotcakes to form a cone, "horn of plenty." Fill each with 1 tbsp. orange hardsauce - chilled before using :   1 cube butter
½ cup powdered sugar
2 oranges - rind and juice
dash of brandy - if desired
Top Orange Cone with another spoonful of hardsauce.

Sourdough Fish Blintz

Use basic
Sourdough recipe.   Add an
extra egg to make very thin batter.
Make thin 6-inch Sourdoughs.
Keep them hot while making filling:

  2 cups flaked fish
  2 cups cottage cheese (dry)
  1 egg
  1 tbsp. grated onion
  salt — pepper — thyme

Spoon cheese-fish mix in center
of each Sourdough hot. Fold edges up
and over like an envelope. Seal edges
with Sourdough batter.

Place Sourdough Fish Blintz in buttered
pan. Brush with butter. Heat thru in oven.

Note: Alaska Smoked Salmon or
Kodiak crab gives delightful taste appeal.

Sourdough Strawberry Roll

To Basic Sourdough Recipe
add one egg - if available.
Bake thin and tender 7-inch hotcake
Dust with powdered sugar.
Cover with thin sliced strawberries
Roll up as for a jelly roll.
Serve hot, with sour cream and berries.

～ ～ ～ ～ ～ ～ ～ ～

Sour Cream Substitute

1 carton cottage cheese
3/4 cup buttermilk

Blend well until smooth.

Incidentally, this has many calories
less than the real – and many like
the taste better.

Ham 'n' Cheese
Sourdoughs

Use basic Sourdough recipe.
Before adding the soda, mix:
   ½ tsp. prepared mustard
   ½ cup chopped ham
   ½ cup grated cheese
Stir well in batter
   Add soda at last minute when
ready to bake the hotcakes.
   Make dollar-sized Sourdoughs

   ...Alternative...
   In regular basic Sourdough
batter dip slices of ham and
cheese. Bake to golden
brown.
   Serve with chili sauce
or spiced cranberries.

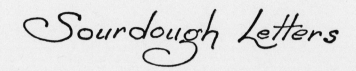

Have you ever eaten your initials? They are delicious! That is, if they are baked Sourdough letters. These are a certain hit with the young fry with a temperamental appetite.

Simply make Sourdough batter — any flavor desired or plain-using the Basic Recipe. From the tip of the spoon, form Sourdough letters on the hot griddle. Turn carefully when brown. Serve hot.

Sourdough Circus

　　Using Basic Recipe for the batter, drip on the griddle various shapes of animals.

　　Or bake separate parts and form the animals on the serving plate. Note how the circle can be the basis for many animals.

　　Your imagination is the limit!

Bits of fruit or bacon used for eyes, ears, tusks, etc.

Sourdough Sam
The
Smilin' Banana Man

Use Basic Sourdough Recipe.

Fold into the Sourdough batter one finely diced banana.

Bake plate-sized hotcakes to a golden brown.

Decorate with slices of banana, making the face with slices for eyes and nose, with a long slice for a grin.

Sourdough Snowman

Dust the Sourdough hotcake—or a stack of hots — with coconut. Add face using banana slices or any fruit available.

The Sourdough Tree

Pancake Tuesday's
centerpiece

Instead of "tying
apples on a lilac tree"
as suggested by the poet — make a
Sourdough Tree out of driftwood or
a branch of willow, and miniature
Sourdough hotcakes!

Select tiny tin lids; thread with fine
wire loops. Dip lids in Sourdough batter.
Bake to golden brown.

Insert a bit of ribbon thru loop,
and tie to the branches in a decora-
tive arrangement.

A wonderful conversational piece.

78

Pancake Tuesday

Pancake Tuesday is a centuries-old traditional holiday.

Also known as Shrove Tuesday or Pancake Day, it is the day before Ash Wednesday - the start of Lent.

The history concerning the pancake pre-dates the day.

Cavemen discovered that grain moistened and baked on stones made a very good food. This was the very beginning of the modern pancake or hotcake.

Pancake Day originated in 1000 A.D. In England, Abbot Aelfrec, set forth a proclamation that "in the week before Lent everyone shall go to his confessor and confess his deeds.

Pancake Tuesday (continued)

The confessor shall so shrive him
as he may then hear by his deeds
what he is to do."

This proclamation resulted in the
wide observance of "Shrove Tuesday."

In old England, at the tolling of the
bell in the morning on Pancake Day, it
was customary for the housewife to drop
whatever she was doing and hurry to
confession. Since this was also a feast
day in small towns — eating pancakes —
the holiday cakes—soon became known
as "Shriving Cakes" because they were
made on the day women were "shriven"
of their sins.

Food Cache
and Cabin near
Fairbanks, Alaska

Sourdough
Bread

Food Cache

Sourdough Bread

Sourdough can be so advantageously used with almost anything fariniceous. With cornmeal, one can create a really memorable johnny bread, better known as corn bread. Cooked rice left over can readily be converted into tasty fritters; the rolled oats you didn't eat for breakfast will work into excellent muffins, if you will give those busy enzymes fuel to work.

Let's say that you are faced with a forty-mile mush. That's a long hike even on a good trail, and you don't want to have to stop for a mid-day meal. Take a couple of hunks of Sourdough bread (the word is used advisedly, for you do not want the wafer-thin slice of the tearoom). Slap between them a thick slab of headcheese made from moose's nose. There you have a meal that can be carried in your own parka pocket.

This will be fuel to keep your boiler going. Pretty hard to find a tastier sandwich, too, if the headcheese was prepared by the recipe of

"Eat-'em-up" Frank, who ran a roadhouse at Tanana.

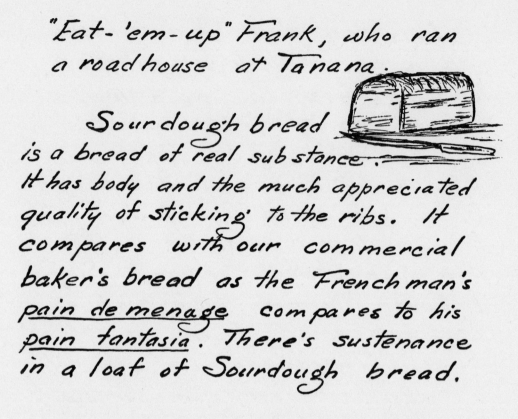

Sourdough bread is a bread of real substance. It has body and the much appreciated quality of sticking to the ribs. It compares with our commercial baker's bread as the Frenchman's _pain de menage_ compares to his _pain fantasia_. There's sustenance in a loaf of Sourdough bread.

Then, of course, there are the Sourdough biscuits, more properly called rolls. They can be run up quickly for the evening meal, and are gustatorially many thousands of enzymes ahead of their baking powder counterparts.

And anyway, even if the baking powder biscuits were better, the Oldtime Alaskan would not include them in his regular diet.

Biscuits are said to have been the bread of the pioneer era. Early day waitresses were called "Biscuit Slingers". Perhaps, those little rounds of bread might have served as a handy defense in their day — but certainly not using Sourdough Biscuits!

One of the pioneer Sourdough doctor's idea of these biscuits was described as follows: "Sourdough biscuits are without a peer. They are so light that a zephyr would

85

pick them up like eiderdown and waft them off in the spring air --- and Sourdough Bread has to be anchored down like a dirigible, or it will blow away in the slightest gust."

Jack often talked about his boyhood in Fairbanks at the turn of the century. "It was my job 50 years ago to freeze bread on baking day! Mother baked 25 to 30 loaves of Sourdough bread at a time. When the bread was ready to take from the oven, I would put on my heavy mitts, pick up the hot pans from the oven, take them out the back door, and toss them into the snow drift." ___ Flash Freeze Service.

With the thermometer ranging
from -20° to -50° during the
winter months in Fairbanks.
Mother Nature provided a simple
quick-freeze. And with no
operating expenses. Immediately
the bread froze before it hit the
snow bank, sealing in all the oven
freshness in each loaf. Nature
had a flash freeze service.
Then, I picked up the loaves of
bread, stacking it like cord wood
on our back porch — in a special
cabinet reserved for frozen bread."

Truly this was a fore runner
of today's deep freeze!
When bread was needed,
a loaf was thawed out slowly.
Usually placed in a paper
bag, brought into the kitchen

and left to thaw out at room temperature. Too much heat too quickly in "defrosting" the bread, caused a soggy crust.... and often the crust to separate from the bread.

Frozen bread was simple to take along when travelling by dog team. Grub always proved a problem. However, a couple of loaves of frozen bread could easily be put in the sack hung on the handle bars of the sled. The cold weather would be no concern as the bread already was frozen.

Today, there are those living out on lone creeks

and isolated places who will stock in their cache their winter supply of bread. It isn't unusual that they have 100 (or even double the number) of frozen loaves of bread in the cache — since there is no convenient "corner bakery" for several hundred miles.

The old Sourdough pioneer used the convenience of the frozen food years before the modern deep freeze became popular in the modern kitchen.

Sourdough Bread

4 cups Sourdough
2 cups warm potato water
½ cup sugar
6 tbsp. cooking oil
1 tsp. salt
10 cups flour - approximately

Make soft sponge mixing the Sourdough, sugar, water and oil. Add half the flour. Set in warm place to double in bulk. Add remainder of flour to make dough that is easy to handle, smooth and elastic. Place in greased bowl. Cover. Let raise in warm place until double in bulk. Knead down. Let raise to double bulk. Form into loaves or roll out ¼" thick. Roll length wise and place on cookie sheet. Slash. Bake 500° for 10 minutes, then 400° for 45 minutes.

Sourdough Bread

QUICK and EASY

1 cup Sourdough
1 pkg. yeast
1½ c. warm water

6 cups flour
2 tbsp. sugar
½ tsp. soda

½ tsp. salt

Add yeast to warm water. Mix in Sourdough, 4 cups of flour, sugar and salt. Beat well. Put in greased bowl and let rise until doubled. Mix soda in 1 cup flour, Add to original dough. Knead until satiny and springy to the touch.

Cut dough in half and make 2 loaves. Bake in 400° oven for 45 minutes

Sourdough Soda Bread

4 cups Sourdough
4 tbsp. oil
2 tbsp. sugar
1 tsp. soda
1 tsp. salt
8-10 cups flour

Mix Sourdough, sugar, shortening together. Add soda dissolved in jigger glass of warm water. Stir well. Add flour, beating with wooden spoon until very thick. Make certain well mixed. If not, it will cause yellow streaks in bread.

Knead in flour to make dough smooth and elastic — not sticky.

Form into loaves and let raise in bread pans to double size. Only raise once. Bake 400° for 30 minutes; reduce to 350° for the remaining 30 minutes.

Sourdough Flower Rolls

1 cup Sourdough
½ cup sugar
1 egg
4 tbsp. cooking oil
½ tsp. soda
1 tsp. baking powder
2 cups flour - or more -

Mix Sourdough with egg, sugar and oil. Fold in dry ingredients, with flour enough to make elastic sponge. Turn out on board. Knead smooth. Put in greased bowl. Cover. Let rise until double in bulk.

Roll out to ¼" thick. Cut 1" circles. Arrange in muffin tin on edge with one in center. Let rise 30-minutes.

Punch down center round with finger. Add filling to center. Bake in 400 oven for 15 minutes.

Filling for Flower Rolls

Cranberry: combine —
  ½ cup cranberry sauce (whole)
  ¼ cup crushed pineapple (drained)
  ½ tsp. orange peel

Prune: mix together —
  1 ½ cups thick puréed prunes
  4 tbsp. sugar
  ½ tsp. lemon peel

Cottage Cheese: blend thoroughly —
  1 cup cottage cheese
  2 egg yolks
  ½ tbsp. melted butter
  ¼ cup sugar
  1 tsp. lemon rind
  1 tsp. vanilla

Marmalades —   Home made Jellies —

Sourdough
Blueberry Muffins

1 cup Sourdough
½ cup sugar
4 tbsp. oil
1 egg
2 cups flour
½ tsp. soda
1 tsp. baking powder
(1 tsp. grated orange or lemon rind)
1 cup blue berries

Mix Sourdough, egg, shortening together. Sift in all dry ingredients. Do not beat but rather fold in, over and over. Add blueberries that have been dusted with flour. Dip into well greased muffin tins. Bake in 400° oven for 25 minutes.
Secret of tender muffins: expediency and unnecessary handling of batter.

Sourdough
Muffins

2 cups Sourdough
½ cup sugar
1 egg
½ cup oil
1 ½ cup flour   (try whole wheat)
1 tsp. soda
(1 cup raisins)

Mix Sourdough, sugar, egg and oil;
add half the flour; then add soda
diluted in a jigger glass warm water.
Add rest of flour along with the
raisins. Do not beat, merely use
folding action, so as not to interrupt
the soda reaction.

Fill greased muffin tins half full.
Bake 375° oven for 30 minutes.

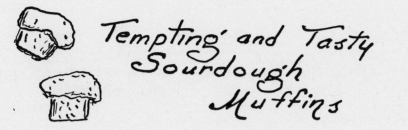
Tempting and Tasty Sourdough Muffins

Corn Meal Muffins

½ cup yellow corn meal. Fill cup with boiling water. Stir after it swells. Add to Sourdough Muffin batter.

Cheese Muffins

¾ cup grated cheese added to Muffin batter. Bake in 8-inch ring mold.

Up-Side-Down Muffins

Add nuts and/or fruit to bottom of well greased muffin tins. Pour in batter.

Muffin "Doughnuts"

Roll hot Muffins in melted butter, then in sugar and cinnamon. Serve hot.

Sourdough English Muffins

Baked on a griddle, using baking rings. Baking rings made by cutting top and bottom out of any squat can. The old prospector cut out his "snoose" tin which made perfect rings.

2 cups Sourdough
½ pkg. Yeast

2 tbsp. sugar
2 tbsp. cooking oil

Flour - enough to make stiff batter.

Dissolve yeast in warm water. Mix into the Sourdough, sugar and oil. Stir in enough flour to make a stiff dough. Cover and set in warm place to raise to spongy dough consistency.

Grease rings and skillet well. Drop 2 tbsp dough in each ring on _hot_ griddle. Flip over when dough is flat with top of tin. After once turned will raise no more. Let brown. Split and serve hot.

Sourdough Pumpernickel

2 cups Sourdough   2 tbsp. oil
2 packages yeast   1 tsp. salt
½ cup molasses
⅔ cup corn meal - fill with boiling water.
4 cups rye flour
1 cup whole wheat flour

Dissolve yeast in ¼ cup warm water; mix into Sourdough with molasses, oil and cornmeal (semi-solid consistency). Work in rye and whole wheat flour. Add extra if necessary.

Place dough in well greased bowl. Cover with damp cloth and let stand 3 hours. Poke down. Knead down 2 times. Form in loaf. Keep warm until double in bulk.

Bake 350° oven for 1½ hours. Remove from pan. Rub with melted butter. Return to oven for 20 minutes - making tender crust.

Sourdough French Bread

2 cups Sourdough
1 tbsp. sugar
1 tbsp. cooking oil
¼ tsp. salt
6 cups flour -- approximately

Make hollow in center of flour, sugar and salt; pour in Sourdough stirring from center to edge, forming soft, smooth and elastic dough. Put out on floured board. Pull out dough and fold over, rather than ordinary kneading — pulling puts in air bubbles. Roll dough out to 10"x 14". Do not spread with butter. Merely roll as a jelly roll. With each roll pinch, sealing in air. Lay roll on greased cookie sheet. Slash with sharp knife. Let raise 3 times original size. (This takes most of day.) Bake 475° for 10 minutes. Paint with cold water. Reduce to 375° for 30 minutes.

Sourdough-Cranberry Pan Rolls

1 cup Sourdough
1 pkg. yeast
1/4 cup. sugar
1 egg   salt

1 cup cranberries (ground)
1/2 cup sugar

Dissolve yeast in 1/4 cup water. Mix into Sourdough, eggs, shortening. Add flour enough to make soft dough. Turn out on floured board. Knead to a smooth satiny texture. Place in greased bowl. Set in warm place until double in bulk. Punch down. Let rise second time.

Mix together 1/3 cup bread crumbs and 1/3 cup brown sugar and 3 tbsp. butter.

Roll dough out to 12"x18" sheet. Spread with cranberry-sugar mixture. Roll up like jelly roll, seal brushing edges with cold water, pinch tight. Cut in 1-inch slices. Spread crumbs in bottom of tin. Let rise again. Bake 350° for 45 minutes.

Alaska's Easter Sourdough Coffee Cake

4 cups Sourdough
2/3 cup Fireweed honey
1 tsp. salt
add: 1 cake yeast
    dissolved in 1/4 cup water.
Mix well. Work in 3 cubes butter.
Add: flour until dough is as thick as
can be beaten with wooden spoon.
    Add: 1 cup blanched almond halves
        1 tsp. grated lemon rind
            green citron to taste
Work in 6 eggs.
Add enough flour that dough is soft but
not sticky. Toss with whipping motion of
hands, kneading to center of bowl.
    Put in 9x9 baking pan. Let it gently
smooth itself into shape. Cover. Let rise to
double in bulk—or more. Top with butter and
honey. Bake in 425° oven

Sourdough Waffles

Definition: (not Webster's)
"A waffle is an enlarged
hotcake with a non-skid tread."

Time was when Waffles were
considered only for a special Sunday Treat,
or something to be served to company.
Today waffles have become a most
popular around-the-clock dish for every

day meals. They are wonderful for luncheon snacks, satisfying as a main course, delicious for dessert, and ever ready for breakfast and brunch.

The old fashioned "black-iron" waffle iron was heavy and a problem to heat. Waffles demanded steady heat and plenty of it. Many exasperating experiences accompanied baking waffles over the wood or coal burning ranges. The cook usually had an extra supply of dry wood or chips on hand to use in keeping a hot fire under the iron. And tinder dry wood wasn't always easy to find. Often times the cook had to go chop extra wood to make

an extra hot fire
for the waffle
iron.

Electricity and the advent of the
heat controlled waffle iron boosted
the popularity of the waffle.

However, an electrical appliance can
provoke problems in the out of the
way places where you have your
own electric plant. It is then you
have to crank up the engine, which
at times proves temperamental, before
you can get "juice" for the iron. It
is amazing how much electricity is needed
to get the iron the desired heat. So,
you find it necessary to turn out
lights here and there to increase the
electrical load for the waffle iron.
And when you get the waffles baked,

they are all worth while
the effort.

Waffles are wonderful to meet an
emergency. They are filling and appeal
to all ages.

One time I served breakfast to a group
of Eskimos who had never tasted Sourdoughs.
When they asked for seconds and thirds it
gave me courage to ask if waffles were as
good as "Ooligan and Fish"! They shook
their heads for nothing — nothing
compares to "Ooligan Oil and Fish"!
But they did compliment the waffles!

When a boatload of tired. hungry
crabfishermen came to our place for
food, the old Sourdough Pot came to the rescue.
It didn't take long to whip up a batch of

waffles, topping them with a rich luscious crab newburg! Apologies about bringing "coals to Newcastle" were not necessary, for the crab fishermen complimented the cook by passing their plates for more, and asking for the recipe.

Sourdough waffles are easy and simple to make. There is no bother of beating egg whites as required in regular waffle recipes. As a matter of fact, the same recipe is used for both Sourdough Hotcakes and Sourdough Waffles. Difference is all in the baking. That little jingle is packed full of truth when it claims "A waffle is an enlarged hotcake with a non-skid tread!"

Basic Recipe
Sourdough Waffles

2 cups Sourdough Starter
2 tbsp. sugar
4 tbsp. cooking oil
1 egg
½ tsp. salt
1 tsp. (scant) soda.

Into Sourdough dump sugar, egg, oil and salt. Mix well. Dilute soda in warm water in jigger glass, stirring with the little finger. Fold soda gently into batter. Do not beat. Stir with easy rhythmic motion turning the spoon. Notice the deep, hollow tone as batter thickens and doubles in volume with bubbles.

Dip batter immediately to hot iron.

Sourdough
Lenten Waffle
Suggestions

To: Basic Sourdough Recipe

Add: ½ cup flaked codfish
        1 tsp. prepared mustard.
Bake waffles to golden brown
Serve: Topping of scrambled eggs
        or Cheese Sauce

o o o o o o o o o o o

To: Basic Sourdough Recipe

Add: 1 can flaked Tuna — or —
        1 cup cut shrimp — or —
        1 cup flaked smoked salmon.
Bake waffles to golden brown.
Sprinkle generously with grated cheese.
Pop under broiler until cheese melts. Serve.

Sourdough
Raisin Waffles

To: Basic Sourdough Recipe

Add: ½ cup seedless raisins – or–
    ½ cup diced dried figs
which have been allowed to come to a
boil. Drain well.
        1 tsp. lemon or orange rind
Bake waffle to golden brown
Serve for dessert with ice cream
with lemon sauce.

○ ○ ○ ○ ○ ○ ○ ○ ○ ○

Banana Waffles

To: Basic Sourdough Recipe
Add: to batter on waffle iron
    bananas cut lengthwise strips
that have been sprinkled with lemon
juice (to prevent discoloring.)
Bake as for regular waffles.

Sourdough Waffle-wiches

Tasty, crunchy Sourdough waffles are the base of these glorified club sandwiches.

Sourdough waffles can be baked ahead, frozen, and popped in toaster or under broiler when ready to use.

Generously fill, with variety of appetizing combinations, between the stacked Sourdough waffles. Serve at the table, cutting thick slices for servings.

Suggestions

<u>Bacon-Tomato-Cheese</u> : Place crisp bacon and sliced tomato between, top with cheese. Put under broiler until cheese melts.

<u>Ham</u> 'n <u>Cheese</u> : Smoked ham spread with prepared mustard. Top with cheese and chili sauce.

Flaming Sourdough Waffle

1 section Sourdough Waffle
1 slab Seward's Ice Box (Ice Cream)
Douse with Wild Strawberries
Dip chunk of Glacier Ice (Sugar Cube)
    into Fire water (Lemon Extract)*
Set aflame!

* Lemon extract will flame <u>cold</u>,
whereas brandy must be heated to flame.

Created for the special celebration
of Alaska Statehood, and raising of the
49 star flag.
Today it is served for tourists at
The House of Wickersham - Juneau.

Spread for Sourdough Appetizers

Alaska Herringchova Paste

Use Alaska herring — pickled, smoked or dried. Remove fat, bones and skin. Chop fine.

    1 cup minced herring
    1/4 cup butter
    1/8 tsp. cayenne pepper
    1/8 tsp. ground cloves

Mix to smooth paste.
A jar tightly covered will keep indefinitely in the refrigerator.

Sourdough Bean Spread

½ cup beans (drained), mashed to pulp.
2 tbsp. minced green onions or chives
    Salad dressing to make smooth paste.
    Salt, pepper to taste

Corned Beef or Venison Spread

½ cup minced corned beef or venison
½ cup minced sweet potatoes
2 tbsp. butter

Cordova Clam Relish Spread

1 can minced clams — drain
1 pkg. cream cheese
2 tbsp. sweet-pickle relish
    Blend well to make smooth paste
Add salt, pepper, Tabasco sauce to taste.
Pickle relish gives very special zest to spread
If prefer, can use : 2 tbsp. chopped pickle - or
                     2 tbsp. minced onion - or
                     2 tbsp. chives chopped fine.

Barbecued Smoked Salmon

½ cup barbecued smoked salmon (drained)
1 tbsp minced green onions
   Salad dressing to make smooth paste
   Salt and pepper to taste. Delicious!

Sourdough
Cocktail Waffles

Wonderful substitute for toast or crackers for hot canapes.

Better, since you can bake your favorite tangy spice right in the waffle.

Make ahead of time; <u>label</u> with the special-spice of the waffle before putting in the freezing unit. Keep a variety on hand for spur of the moment needs. Store whole waffle. Do not cut until ready to use.

Excellent way to utilize left over batter from morning Sourdoughs.

Add to the batter - a dash of
   curry powder   or
   chili powder   or
   mustard and horse radish

116

Use only enough for a hint rather than overpowering use of these pungent spices.

All Alaskan
Appetizers

Appetizers: Something to eat to make you hungrier than you are when you are hungry.

Alaskan appetizers are popular conversational tid-bits — simple for the hostess to prepare — exciting taste appeal.

Suggested Taste Teasers

Sourdough Canapes — hot waffle wedges squares or wheels.

Squaw Candy — hard smoked Yukon salmon.

Kelp Life Savers - circle around nippy cheese.

Pickled Herring - bite sized bits

Marinated Shrimp -

Alaska Crab Claws -

Jerky - dried caribou or reindeer

Muk-tuk - Eskimo - delicacy if you go Native!

117

The Sourdough Dessert
Baked Alaska

Baked Alaska! Ice Cream popped in a hot oven and coming out unscarred from its baptism of terrific heat. This has come to be known today as Baked Alaska.

Quite an international history hovers around this unique dessert.

At the turn of the century there was a discovery that the albumen - "eggwhite" - could be used as insulation from heat

An American physicist made the startling discovery that stiffly beaten egg whites would prevent penetration of heat. This idea excited culinary artists and many experiments were made with the meringue.

1867 - French chef had to prepare a state dinner honoring American dignitaries in Paris. The topic of the hour was, "Seward's Ice Box."

Very facetiously, the chef created an Ice dessert - encased in meringue - and baked. He called it: "Omelette Surprise" Today we know it as, "Baked Alaska"!

Sourdough
Baked Alaska

Items Needed:

Sourdough Waffle - Crisp

Ice Cream - Brick or Bulk

Meringue - fluffy and dry

Wooden Plank — never use metal or
crockery as they conduct heat.

Hot Oven - 500°

Place crisp, crunchy waffle on board — bread board is excellent to use.

For oblong waffle, place slab of ice cream leaving 1-inch border of waffle all around. For round waffle, pack bulk ice cream in a bowl, leaving a 1-inch margin of waffle all around. Do not use Sherbet or any Ices.

Completely seal in ice cream with swirls of glossy dry meringue. Since the egg whites are an insulation, make certain that meringue tightly prevents any heat getting in to melt the ice cream.

Place the Baked Alaska in very hot oven - 500°. Leave oven door open a crack. Remove when meringue is delicate brown.

Quickly slip to chilled plate or platter. Serve immediately.
Hot and soft outside! Cool and firm inside and Delicious to eat!
Sourdough Baked Alaska.

Sourdough
Birthday Cake

"Aurora"
Baked Alaska

1 Sourdough Waffle - crisp
and crunchy— lemon, orange
coconut flavored - or just
plain waffle well baked.

1 Quart Ice cream - well frozen—
strawberry, mint, tutti frutti
or vanilla — just so its hard.

Meringue Frosting   6-8 egg whites.
Have plenty of fluffy dry meringue.

Candles - egg shells filled with
brandy and set aflame.

Meringue

Baked Alaska

6 egg whites
1 cup sugar
1/2 tsp. cream of tartar

Whip egg whites until dry and stiff,
forming peaks that will stand alone.
Very slowly add the sugar, beating
until smooth and glossy. If not beaten
enough <u>before</u> sugar is added, the
meringue will <u>not</u> get stiff enough to
hold shape regardless of later beating.
Flavoring: Make taste-appealing as
well as eye-appealing. A drop of creme de
menthe gives delicate peppermint flavor,
creating billows of sea foam colored
meringue One drop of vegetable coloring
transforms the snow white mounds into

Meringue - continued

blushing pink peaks. Caution: it takes very small drop of coloring or extract to satisfy both taste appeal and eye appeal.

To Bake: Preheat oven 500° Speed in baking operation is a necessity. Watch oven constantly. Let the Alaska remain in oven only long enough for meringue to be tinted a delicate brown.

Baked Alaska
au
Flambé

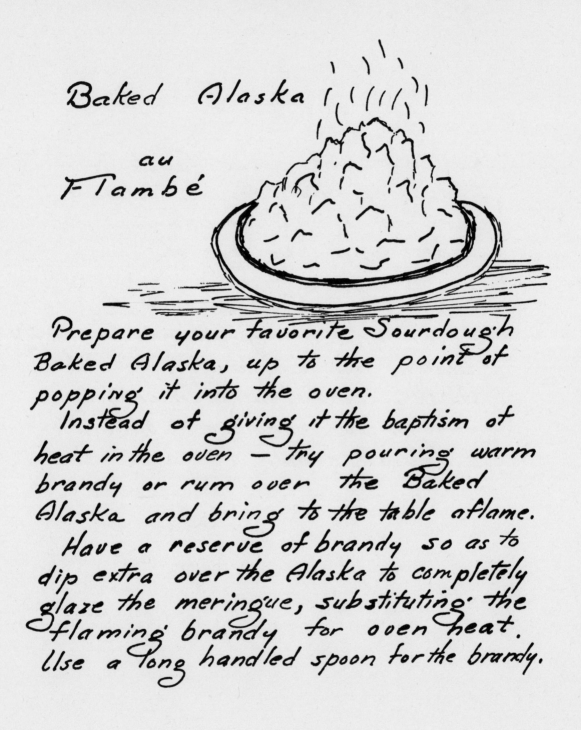

Prepare your favorite Sourdough Baked Alaska, up to the point of popping it into the oven.

Instead of giving it the baptism of heat in the oven — try pouring warm brandy or rum over the Baked Alaska and bring to the table aflame.

Have a reserve of brandy so as to dip extra over the Alaska to completely glaze the meringue, substituting the flaming brandy for oven heat. Use a long handled spoon for the brandy.

Northern Lights
Baked Alaska.

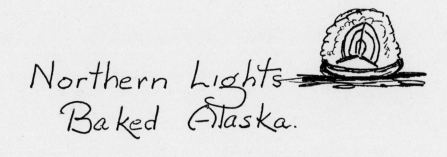

Packing the Ice cream secret for this
unusual to the eye and taste.
2 pints pistachio Icecream
1 pint strawberry Icecream
½ pint vanilla Ice cream.

Refrigerate 1½ qt. bowl. Soften slightly the
pistachio Icecream by putting from freezer to the
refrigerator. With large spoon press pistachio
Ice cream evenly around sides of bowl. Then
press Strawberry Icecream around. Fill
center with Vanilla Icecream. Place in freezer
over night to make very firm for ite
           Baked Alaska.

Individual Baked Alaska

Popular dessert...
Easy to make ...
Simple to serve ...
No muss or fuss in serving

   Cut crisp Sourdough waffle in desired segments — square, oblong, round, diamond. Place waffle on wood-board. Top with scoop or slab of hard ice cream.
   Hollow out a well in the ice cream. Fill with fresh or preserved fruit — peach, pineapple preserve, strawberry or blue berries.
   Completely seal with swirls of meringue. Bake in 500° oven 2 to 5 minutes until points of meringue are delicate brown.
   For Birthday dessert — decorate with an egg shell cup. Fill with brandy after removing from oven. The heated shell makes lighting of "candle" simple.

128

Pineapple Baked Alaska

Pineapple slices - well drained
Sourdough waffles
Ice cream   -   Meringue

Trim Sourdough waffles to size of the
pineapple rings. Drain pineapple dry.
Chill. Place on waffle rings. Arrange
on wood board. Completely cover with
swirls of meringue. Put on garnish
of slivers of toasted almonds and coconut.
Brown in 500° oven 2 to 5 minutes, or
until delicate brown.
Serve quickly.
        ...Substitute...
Peach halves - drained dry are excellent
to use in lieu of pineapple. Fruit must
be dry or dessert will become soggy.

Baked Alaska - Fruit Brick -

Crisp Sourdough Waffle
    2 or 3 square units
Strawberry Icecream
    quart brick
Meringue - mint flavor
    Frozen Strawberries
    Place Sourdough waffle sections on
wood board.
    Cut brick of strawberry ice cream
lengthwise, making 2 or 3 slabs, as
you desire size of Fruit Brick.
    Add a layer of frozen strawberries
between slabs of ice cream.
    Cover entire brick with meringue,
which has been flavored and colored with
a drop of creme de menthe. This gives
a beautiful contrast.
    Bake in 500° oven until delicate brown.
Serve immediately.

Baked Alaska Igloo

Crisp 9" round Sourdough waffle.
Ice cream — 1 pint each vanilla,
    strawberry and chocolate.
Meringue —

Pack ice cream in round salad mold
or bowl, arranging spoonfuls of each
flavor to make marbled effect. Chill.

Arrange Sourdough waffle on wood
board. Put mound of ice cream on the
waffle, leaving margin of waffle clear.

Use a cube of ice cream for entrance.

Cover entirely with meringue, smooth
and shape with spatula. Line with
toothpick dipped in melted bitter chocolate.
Dust meringue well with sugar. Set in
500° oven to brown delicately. Serve.

Sourdough Marriage Contract
(carved on birch tree during one of the early Alaskan Stampedes)

Ten miles from the Yukon
On the banks of this lake,
A partner to Koyukuk
McGillis, I take;
We have no preacher ---
We have no ring ---
It makes no difference
It's all the same thing.
 (signed) Aggie Dalton.

I swear by my Gee-pole,
Under this tree,
A faithful husband to Aggie
I always will be;
I'll love and protect her
This maiden so frail,

Sourdough Marriage Contract
(continued)

From the Sourdough bums
On the Koyukuk Trail.
    (signed) Frank McGillis

For two dollars a-piece
In "cheechako" money,
I unite this couple
In matrimony;
He be a rancher
She be a teacher
I do up the job
Just as well as a preacher.
    (signed) French Joe

Sourdough

Doughnuts
Cakes
Cookies

Sourdough
Cakes...Doughnuts...Cookies

According to Webster's dictionary, a cake is "a small mass of dough baked."

Tastes have changed as well as the techniques for baking a cake or a batch of cookies. Environment and circumstances are a determining factor in developing many an unusual recipe.

Alaskan pioneers overcame some impossible hurdles to produce tasty cakes and cookies.

Salt was a real
premium commodity
during the Chisana Stampede. No
corner grocery for miles around.
Jack considered himself very
lucky to "get a handful of salt—
just enough to tie in a silk
handkerchief." Price: $2.50 in
gold dust.

Eggs proved to be a very difficult
necessity. An item in Alaska's first
newspaper, the Yukon Press, published
at Circle City, January 15, 1899, reads
"John Snell of California arrived at Rampart
last fall with a large cargo of eggs.
Constant worry over the perishableness
of his cargo led him to commit suicide!"

Eskimos use the Eider duck egg for
food. They gather them, and hide them

under rocks away from the
direct rays of the sun. By September
they are frozen, and they put them away
for their winter use. This is one
way of having fresh eggs all winter.

One of Juneau's outstanding
cooks jokes about the cakes that were
baked at Katalla during the early
boom days. No eggs available in town,
the resourceful pioneer wife substi-
tuted sea gull eggs. The cakes
baked with these eggs had a distinct
and disagreeable piscatorial flavor
that could not be disguised. Today
it is a laughing matter — but
then, those "fishy cakes" were not
a joke.
Frozen eggs proved a challenge for

the best of the pioneer cooks, whether making a cake or just cooking the breakfast eggs.

The Alaskan native readily acquired a taste for the white man's butter. He liked the salty taste — something different from his native foods and he would make great efforts to get some "Gleese."

Butter and lard were a problem for the cook. They were not only hard to carry on the trail, they were often so rancid upon arrival they couldn't be used.

Meeting such problems established the old Sourdough as a skillful and versatile cook. He found out that processing bear fat with boiling water eliminated the obnoxious smell and taste of lard rendered from old bruin. Caution had to be used: "Drip bear fat into boiling water. Do Not Pour! Water sputters and splatters. Danger of serious burns. But the efforts are rewarding, as the bear fat becomes clear white and tasteless!" It could be used for deep frying or for pastry, cakes or cookies.

Fried cakes and doughnuts really were appreciated because enough lard for deep frying was so hard to get.

The native Eskimo and Indian used ooligan oil or seal oil for cooking. or as a preservative. However, this oil has a strong taste for the white man.

Watching the white man, the native has been initiated into the doughnut-dunkers'-department — and likes it!

Sourdough Doughnuts

"A cross between cake and raised doughnut — half 'n' half."

1 cup thick, rich Sourdough
1 egg
1 tbsp. cooking oil
1 cup sugar
1 tsp. nutmeg
1 tsp. cinnamon
½ tsp. soda
2 tsp. baking powder
½ tsp. salt
2 cups flour — or enough to make soft dough easy to handle.

Pour Sourdough in bowl with egg, shortening and all dry ingredients. Do not handle more than necessary.

Let stand after cutting to allow doughnut to puff up before frying in 375° deep fat.

Makes 2 dozen doughnuts for a "mug up."

Chocolate Sourdough Links

Divide into 2 portions
Sourdough doughnut
recipe. To one portion add:
   1 square unsweetened chocolate (melted)
in 2 tbsp. milk over hot water.

   Roll both mixtures of dough to
¼-inch thick.
   Cut with standard doughnut cutter.
   Clip chocolate doughnut and link
through plain doughnut. Seal
pinching together.
   Cover to let puff up before
frying in deep oil - 375°
   Drain on paper towel.

Sourdough Twisters

Follow recipe for Sourdough
doughnuts— any flavor.
  Roll dough out to ½-inch thickness.
  Cut in strips 1-inch wide 8-inch
long.
  Twist several turns.
  Cover, and let puff up.
  Drop in 375° deep oil; fry to brown.
  Dust with sugar or glaze.

Sourdough Tea Balls

Prepare Sourdough doughnut dough.
Add 1 tbsp. grated lemon rind.
  Roll out dough to ¼ inch thick.
  Cut in tiny rounds — or use "holes"
from standard-sized doughnuts.
  Fry to golden brown in 375° hot oil.
  Sprinkle with powdered sugar.

Orange Sourdough Drops

½ cup thick Sourdough
⅓ cup sugar
1 egg
2 tbsp. cooking oil
2 tbsp. grated orange rind
1 tsp. nutmeg
2 tsp. baking powder
¼ tsp. soda
½ tsp. salt

To the Sourdough add sugar, egg and oil. Mix well. Add dry ingredients with orange rind. Blend. Do not over beat. Dough soft and easy to drop from spoon. To prevent dough from sticking, dip in hot oil. Use one teaspoon to push dough from other spoon into the hot deep fat - 375.° Fry to golden brown. Drain. Dip in Honey Glaze and roll in coconut.

Icings - Glazes - Frostings
for Sourdough Doughnuts

Cherry Icing :
  1 cup confectioners sugar
  1 tbsp. soft butter
  1 tbsp. milk
     minced maraschino cherries
Mix to a smooth paste. Generously
sprinkle with cherry flecks.

Fireweed Honey Glaze :
  Bring to a boil—
  1/2 cup Fireweed honey
  4 tsp. boiling water
  1 cup powdered sugar
  1 cup shredded coconut.
Take tongs and dip doughnuts
in the glaze.
Roll in coconut.

Carmel Frosting

½ cup butter
1 cup brown sugar
¼ cup milk
2 cups powdered sugar

Mix butter and sugar; boil 2 minutes over low heat. Add milk; stir until it comes to a boil. Slowly add sugar beating hard until thick enough to spread.

Chocolate - Rum Coating

2 tbsp. butter
2 squares chocolate (unsweetened)
2 tbsp boiling water
1 cup powdered sugar.
1 tsp. rum.

Melt butter and chocolate over hot water. Blend in sugar, water and rum. Beat with spoon until smooth.

Sourdough Fried Apple Sauce Cakes

Mix Sourdough Doughnut dough.
Roll very thin — ¼ inch.
Cut with 3-inch circle cutter.
Place apple sauce mix in center,
Moisten edges with water. Cap with another
circle. Seal tight pinching with fork.
Fry in 375° hot oil until golden brown.
Garnish with citron leaves and cloves.

Apple Sauce Filling

1 cup cooked apple sauce (thick)
¼ cup brown sugar
¼ cup raisins
1 tsp. lemon juice and grated rind.
½ tsp. cinnamon
½ tsp. nutmeg
1 tbsp. butter (melted)
Mix well.

Sourdough
Chocolate Cake

1 cup Sourdough
1 cup sugar
½ cup cooking oil
2 eggs   1 cup milk
3 squares chocolate (melted)
½ tsp. salt   2 tsp. vanilla
1 tsp. soda   1 tsp. baking powder
   1 cup flour* add if Sourdough is thin.

To Sourdough mix in sugar, oil, eggs.
Add milk and vanilla. Add chocolate
melted over hot water. Stir well but
do not beat hard. Fold in soda and
baking powder at the very last. Actio
starts and batter starts puffing and doubl
ing. Flour is needed only when Sourdough
used is thin. Bake in 9-inch tins 30 —
minutes in 350° oven.

Sourdough Fruit Cake

2 cups Sourdough
2 eggs
2 cups sugar
2/3 cup shortening
2 cups flour (approximately)
1 tsp. cinnamon and nutmeg
1 tbsp. grated lemon peel
1 cup seedless raisins
1 cup fruit cake mix
1 tsp. baking powder
1 tsp. soda dissolved in ½ cup hot water
¼ cup fruit juice or brandy

Cream sugar and shortening; add beaten eggs. Stir in Sourdough and dry ingredients. Dust fruits with flour before stirring into batter. Add soda last, gently folding rather than beating. Bake in 2 loaf tins for 2 hours in 275° oven.

Orange Cup Fruit Cakes

Boil well-cleaned orange shells in clear water until tender.

For special interest, clip notches around edge of orange shell.

Boil again 10 minutes in syrup:

    1 cup water

    2 cups sugar

Remove shells from syrup. Drain.

Roll in sugar. Dry oranges by inverting over coffee cup to retain shape.

Fill orange shell with Sourdough fruit cake dough, to ½ inch of top.

Bake in slow oven, 250°, for 1 hour.

Truly distinctive taste for the fruit cake and orange shell becomes
the Individual
Sourdough Fruit Cake.

Sourdough Soft Ginger Cookies

½ cup Sourdough
½ cup black strap molasses
½ cup shortening
3/4 cup sugar
1 egg
3 ½ cups flour — more or less
2 tsp. ginger
2 tsp. cinnamon
1 tsp. cloves
½ tsp. cardamon
2 tsp. grated orange (lemon) peel
1 tsp. soda

Cream sugar and shortening. Add molasses, egg and orange rind. Mix in Sourdough. Add dry ingredients. Use enough flour to make soft dough. Chill the dough. Roll out on floured board. Cut. Bake on greased cookie sheet 375° 10 minutes.

Sourdough Currant Cookies

1 cup Sourdough
1 cup brown sugar
1 cup cooking oil
1 egg
1 cup all-bran
2 cups white flour - approximately
1 cup currants - or raisins -
      or prunes cut fine
1 tsp. cinnamon
½ tsp. cloves
½ tsp. nutmeg
1 tsp. soda
½ tsp. salt

Mix Sourdough with sugar, egg and shortening. Add flour and spices. Dust the currants with flour before mixing in the batter. Stir well. Do not beat. Drop by spoonsful on baking sheet. Bake in 400° oven for 10 minutes.

Blueberry
Sourdough Dumpling

3 cups blueberries
½ cup boiling water
1 cup sugar
½ tsp. nutmeg and cloves
Boil 5 minutes in heavy skillet
or saucepan with tight fitting cover,
before dropping in small dumplings.

½ cup Sourdough
1 tbsp. sugar
1 tbsp. cooking oil
1 egg   1 tsp. grated lemon rind
1 cup flour
½ tsp. soda   ½ tsp. baking powder
Berry mixture must continue boiling
after dumplings are added. Keep lid tight.
Turn down heat for 12 minutes. Do not
lift lid during cooking period.

Cranberry
Sourdough Steam Pudding

Mix Alaska lowbush cranberries with equal amount of sugar.

Put in well-buttered bowl, in which the pudding is to be steamed.

Spread Sourdough dumpling dough over the cranberries.

1 cup Sourdough
4 tbsp. sugar
4 tbsp. butter
1 egg
1 tsp. cinnamon and nutmeg
1/2 tsp. salt
1/2 tsp. baking powder
1/2 tsp. soda

Tie pudding bag over top of bowl. Place in boiling water, having water 2/3 up on the bowl. Cover lightly. Boil vigorously 30 minutes. Serve on platter.

Syrups and Sauces for Sourdoughs

Syrups and Sauces
for
Sourdoughs

Old time Alaskans are partial to the use of home made products as a dressing for their Sourdoughs. Preserved wild strawberry, salmonberry, red and black huckleberry, nagoon-berry, and blueberry are among the favorites. Once I had a stack of Sourdoughs doused with good home-made Alaska Birch Syrup that compared favorably with Vermont's Maple product.

Alaska Birch Syrup

Alaska's beautiful native birch holds a potential for syrup as popular as its down east cousin.
Years ago an old Sourdough needed drinking water badly on his homestead near Fairbanks. He recalled as a boy in Sweden he had tapped birch in the spring and drank the sap. So, he began to tap Alaska birch on his 160 acres. He found the trees produced a sap slightly sweet with very pleasing aroma. Experimenting further he boiled it down, resulting in a crystal, clear syrup

which was delicious on his stack of Sourdough hotcakes.

Birch contains such elements as calcium, magnesium, iron, potassium, sulphate, and phosphate which makes it a real Spring Tonic!

But it takes time and patience to make birch syrup. Drop by drop the clear liquid fills the bucket— but it takes about 60 buckets of sap to make one gallon of syrup.

Alaska Blueberry Syrup

Blueberries have been an important source of food supply for the Alaskan Indian as well as for the pioneer. Many a legend has been told about these berries. Today's modern housewife uses these native berries in many delicious recipes.

The ultimate topping for a pagoda of rich brown Sourdoughs is made from our wild Alaska blueberries.

In the fall, take a ten or twenty gallon whiskey keg, knock

out one end, and without washing it, put in a layer of sugar about two inches deep. Follow this with about three inches of big, juicy Alaska blueberries.

Repeat this until the keg is full. Cover and store away in the corner of your cabin. Without mashing or a disturbance of any kind, a mild form of fermentation takes place. Those busy little enzymes are working again. In a short time the skins and the seeds have settled to the bottom, and the balance of the keg is filled with a rich, purple cordial.

Spread some of this over your stack of Sourdoughs. You are in for a treat. The bouquet is heady and the flavor something out of this world.

Uncooked Blueberry Jam

1 part blueberries
2 parts sugar

Stir four or five times a day for four days. Seal in jars.

This will keep indefinitely — that is if you can keep it away from those wanting to use it on their morning Sourdough hots.

Spiced Blueberry Jam

Boil for 2 minutes:
4 cups blueberries
7 cups sugar
1 tsp. cloves and cinnamon
Juice of one lemon

"Alaska Strawberries"

The old Alaskan prospector facetiously tried to kid himself into enjoying his monotonous diet of pay-streak bacon and beans-beans-beans. He called them: Alaska Strawberries!

Years ago, when the only travel to Alaska was by boat, one of the highlights of the trip was the midnight supper in the ship's dining room. Alaska Strawberries would top the menu. Many a cheechako (newcomer) could not understand when they ordered Alaska <u>Strawberries</u>, the waiter served a plate of <u>Beans</u>!"

161

Dried Strawberries

An old, old Thlinget Indian recipe.

Boil wild strawberries down to the consistency of heavy, thick paste.

Pour out in 2-inch strips to dry. Store the slabs away in a dry place until needed.

When hungry for some strawberries for breakfast, just whittle off a hunk from this "plug of Shahwk". Soak fruit shaving over night in water. Heat thru in the morning. Serve for breakfast.

A 2-inch square of dried "Shahwk" would make one quart of "fresh" strawberries.

· · · · · ·

The delicate waxy petaled blossom of the wild strawberry is a perfect stand-in for the traditional orange blossoms. Only thing lacking s the pungent sweetness, when used in a wedding corsage.

Alaska Wild Strawberries

The Alaska wild strawberry is tops in taste appeal. Smaller and not as red as the cultivated variety, yet much sweeter. The wild strawberry is found over the country as far as the Arctic. It is packed with energy. One-half cup equals one orange for Vitamin C content.

When Jack and I were "taken into the tribe" by our Thlinget neighbors, we were given a 4-hour Potlatch (party). Shahwk (wild strawberries) were served on this auspicious occasion, a refreshment worthy of the honor.

Southeastern Indians preserved Shahwk in dry slabs for winter food supply.

Wild Strawberry Jam

Equal parts – strawberries
and sugar.
Juice of 1 lemon
Boil slowly until desired thickness.
Seal hot in sterilized jars.
        Excellent for Sourdoughs

Alaska
Wild Strawberry

Strawberry – Pineapple Preserves

6 cups strawberries
6 cups sugar
1 can crushed pineapple
1 lemon – juice and rind.
    Boil slowly until desired thickness.
Seal in sterilized hot jars.

Salmonberry Preserve

1 cup Salmonberries
1 cup sugar

Pick berries when red
and soft, before they turn
salmon yellow.

Combine sugar and berries. Let
stand a few hours. Put over heat
and boil 15 minutes. Take berries
out and boil juice 20 minutes alone.

Return berries to juice.
Pack in sterilized jars. Seal.

o o o o o

Salmonberries are a good "filler".
Combine with other berries, since
they do not have a strong distinctive
taste, as blueberries, strawberries, etc.

Nagoon Berry

The choice berry of Alaska, but unfortunately not available in large quantities.

Makes a superior jelly, outstanding in flavor as well as a beautiful clear red color.

The pioneer housewife would save her supply of Nagoonberry jelly for very special occasions.

No better complement for your Sourdoughs - hots, waffles or biscuits.

Nagoonberry Jelly

4 cups juice
7 cups sugar
1 bottle Certo
Bring to a boil — add Certo — bring to a rolling boil for 1 minute. Pour in glasses.

Alaska Lowbush Cranberry

4 cups lowbush cranberry
4 cups sugar
   Pick berries after the first frost. Wash berries and place in kettle. Do not add water. Keep stirring until berries begin to boil. Then add sugar. When desired consistency put in jars. Seal.

Spiced Lowbush Cranberries

2 cups sugar
4 cups cranberries
1 cup water
1 tsp. cloves
2 sticks cinnamon
1 lemon - juice and grated rind
   Cook slowly without cooking until skins pop open.
   Add 1/2 bottle Certo. Pour in jars.

Soapberry

Looks like Meringue, but is Soapberries beaten to dry peaks!

1 Large bowl
1 tbsp. crushed Soapberries.
1 cup water + more as needed.
Sprinkle envelope "Kool Aide" (flavor)

Soapberries canned in glass jars and water.

To 1 spoonful of berries add 1 cup cold water, and beat. Indians would beat with hand, using rhythmic beat from shoulders. Today's electric beater shortens the process; Add extra water until the bowl is filled with dry peaks.

Chief would end the Potlatch by calling for Soapberries to be served!

Laboratory analysis reports Soapberry to be like the albumen of the egg - Protein.

Long Sugar Syrup

Heat slowly:
 3 parts molasses
 1 part butter
Serve hot over Sourdoughs.

The Alaskan native was very
curious about the slow-running
sweet-stuff the white man used.
He liked it for it tasted so good.

He started calling it "Long Sugar."
We call it Molasses.

Orange - Honey - Butter

Heat over a flame
   ½ cup Fireweed honey
   ½ cup brown sugar
   2 tbsp. butter
   1 orange - grated rind and juice.
Serve as a hot-dip for hotcakes.

Lemon - Rum - Honey

Heat in top of double boiler.
   1 cup honey
   ¼ cup butter
   1 tsp. lemon juice
   1 tbsp. rum.
Mix well. Serve warm.

Rosehips 'n' Sourdough

It is most interesting to note that the Evolution of the Rose predates Man!

A guest at our home, enjoying a meal of Sourdoughs and Roses, complimented me on the tasty Rose condiments on the table. Father John Anderson of Las Cruces, New Mexico, said that they have now traced the Rose to be 32,000,000 years old, compared to Man (upright) only 1,000,000 years old!

Any delicate 5 petal flower is a descendant of the rose. The apple blossom has 5 delicate petals, likewise the peach, pear, strawberry, raspberry — all are a direct offspring of the parent Rose.

Color or size does not change the
lineage. But texture does.
        The orange has 5 petals, but
they are waxy and cup-shaped —
same as the lemon and lime blossoms.
They belong to the citrus family.
        Rose - delicate and flat.
        Citrus - waxy and cup shape.
But they all contain "Vitamin C"
and the Rose has the greatest content.
of the famed Vitamin "C".
        "Rosehips", the fruit of the Rose
resembles miniature apples. Red, round or
olive shaped, it has a core with seeds just
like its descendant-apple. Sometimes,
they are called "Rose apples", others call
them "Rose Haws", the fruit of the Rose. In
Germany and Switzerland "Hagenbutton"
is the name of this popular fruit of the Hedge
Rose found everywhere — their wild Rose.

Mother Nature has a way
of caring for her own.
Down through the ages
animals as well as man have
used the Rose for food.
History records Cleopatra
using "Roses" to keep from tiring.
Today we know "Vitamin C" gives energy.
Returning from vacation, we were amazed
to discover the bears had completely
skinned our wild Rose hedge of Rosehips.
More men died of scurvy than
accidents during the early days of the
Alaskan prospector — scurvy a disease
caused by lack of fresh fruits and Vitamin C.
The old Sourdough in desperation
started to eat the wild Roses — both petals
and the fruit, Rosehips. He found this
combated the dreaded Scurvy.

Oranges or any citrus fruit were difficult for Alaskan prospectors to get. Often when the fruit arrived it would be frozen, and when available the price prohibitive. During the Klondike they were worth their weight in gold — $18.00 per dozen!

The interior of Alaska has miles and acres of the wild rose. There are 5 different varieties, but all loaded with Vitamin "C" compared to the rose of the southern 48 states. The farther north the Rose, the greater Vitamin Content — also the farther north the greater the difficulty to obtain the citrus fruits! The dear Lord had His arm around us to provide the abundance of Vitamin "C".

Rosehips can be eaten raw like an apple, slithered over salads or any breakfast cereals. Use any way you would use an apple – raw or cooked.

Low in pectin, by adding juice and rind of a lemon it makes delicious jelly, jam, marmalade or even ketchup. Rosehips have a delicate flavor like the rose itself.

Remember 3 Roses have the same Vitamin "C" as an Orange — also the greatest natural source of Ascorbic Acid. When you buy Vitamin "C" tablets at the drug store, look for the very very fine print: "Base, Northern European Rosehip," is usually noted.

Rose Hip Soup

Boil whole Rosehips in a lot of water until soft. Put thru a sieve to make a thick puree. Add a wee bit of salt and sugar to make slightly sweet. Serve hot with a dab of whipped cream and shaved almonds.

Rose Hip Syrup
...Fresh Fruit...

Gather rosehips when firm and bright red color, usually after first frost.

Clean, snipping off bothends. Cut fine.

Put rosehips in enamel or glass pan, and not a metal dish.

Cover fruit with water. Bring to a boil.

Cook until tender and easily mashed with wooden spoon.

Strain through fine sieve, or use jellybag to make a perfectly clear juice.

Return pulp to enamel dish. Add water. Boil for 10 minutes. Strain. Combine juices.

Measure. Add equal amount of sugar and juice of lemon to rosehip juice.

Boil for 5 minutes to right consistency. Bottle while hot. Seal immediately

Did you know that:

A couple of spoonsful of Rosehip Syrup added to a tall glass of milk makes a tasty drink.

Rose hips were free for the finding! _Farther north the Rose, greater the Vitamin C content._

The natives of Alaska have used the rose hip as a source of food for years, calling it "Nee-Chee". Tea made from it is stimulating and enjoyable.

During World War II, England gathered 2,000 Tons of rose hips to take the place of citrus fruits, the first food casualty of the war. Rose hips provided England's children a worthy substitute for oranges.

The northern wild rose often supplies a bumper crop of rosehips, measuring up to one-inch in diameter. Truly an easy winter's supply of vitamins. They can be stored in a dark cool place without losing their nutritive value.

Sitka Rose Honey

Honey - without the aid of the Bees!

Boil to 232°   5 lbs. sugar
                6 cups water
Then add lump of alum - size of cherry.
Boil 4 minutes.
Remove from heat.

Add: 24 Sitka Wild Rose blossoms
             (or 8 double rose blossoms)
          24 White Clover blossoms
          12 Red Clover blossoms
Stir well until blossoms all wilted.
Let stand 10 minutes; stir frequently.
Strain.   If you wish to tint to a
light pink, add food coloring with a petal.
Seal while hot in half pint jars.

Rose petal honey was a
popular breakfast item served
by Martha Washington. To assure
a good supply, there was a
special rose garden cultivated
at Mt. Vernon

From an Alaskan Indian woman
I learned the art of combining
wild rose petals with wild strawberries.

Wild Rose Jelly

Bring to a boil ½ cup fresh straw-
berry juice and 2 cups water.
Pour over 1 quart wild rose petals.
Boil 15 minutes. Strain thru jelly bag.
Add 3½ cups sugar; mix well.
Add a drop of red coloring (if desired)
Bring to rolling boil. Add ½ bottle pectin.
Boil hard 1 minute. Pour into glasses.
Cover with paraffin immediately.

Wild Rose Leaf Bouquet

The Alaska Wild Rose has rich green foliage. Before the winter frost, cut the green branches. Put in vase of water to which you have added Glycerine. This preserves the leaves for a Thanksgiving green bouquet — and is a real beauty when the garden is covered with snow.

Pickled Rosehips
(same as pickled crabapples!)

Clean Rosehips, cutting off blossom but leave the stems.

Pack in pint jars.

Bring pickling syrup to heavy boil.
    6 c. vinegar — 8 c. brown sugar
    2 tsp. whole cloves — 6 sticks of cinnamon.

Pour over Rosehips immediately and Seal the jars while hot.

Wonderful served with wild game.

Rosehip Butter

Remember the Rose is the same as the Apple — So make Rosehip Butter same way.

1. Boil Rosehips (that have been cleaned of blossom and stems) in water until soft. Put through colander to remove the seeds. Measure pulp. Add 4 times amount Sugar. Put over low heat. Stir constantly to keep from burning. When satiny and smooth seal in jars.

2. Grind dried Rosehips to fine powder or get commercially made Rosehip powder.
Add Apple Juice to make heavy thick syrup. Beat in 4 times amount Sugar. Boil very slowly. Stir constantly to keep from burning. Seal in jars when right consistency.
Rosehip butter has distinctive taste without extra spices!

Why not try a Spoonful o' Roses?

1. 1 tbsp. Rosehip Powder + Sugar to use in place of cinnamon-sugar on Sourdough waffles — muffins - cereal.

2. 1 tbsp. Rosehip Powder mixed with a cup of Instant Cocoa. This adds a new taste dimension to the regular chocolate or cocoa.

3. 1 tbsp. Rosehip Powder to gravy. Helps to eliminate the "wild tang" of game.

4. 1 tbsp. Rose Hip Powder to give extra flavor to cakes, waffles, muffins or any and all Sourdough hotcakes.

First Aid with Roses

The beautiful Rose can
become a medical assistant!
To combat Poison Oak
make a poultice of sliced Rosehips.
Miles away from a doctor,
an old Indian's remedy prevented
blood poisoning from developing
from a rusty nail thru my foot.
Cleansing the wound with
Kerosene, he then kept fresh
Rosehip poultices on the foot.
constantly changing to keep it fresh.
Three days later the Doctor
said that this was best possible remedy.
Rosehips contain Ascorbic Acid in
unadulterated form — popularly known
as Vitamin "C". Indians use this for all cuts.

Sourdough . . . . .
Hints . . . .

Sourdough Hints

1. You cannot spoil Sourdough!
It is a wild yeast — a ferment. But it
demands attention to be kept working.

2. If it separates, water forming on
top, just stir well and add fuel (flour)
to a smooth batter again.

3. Dip the Sourdough into a bowl to
make your batter. Do not mix in the
Sourdough Pot, as there must be a
Starter to build new Sourdough supply.

4. Leave about 1 cup of Sourdough
for a Starter. If by accident all the

Sourdough is used — do not panic!
Just add flour and water and scrape
down sides of the Sourdough Pot.
There will be enough enzymes to start
the Sourdough to bubble again.

5. Never add flour when mixing
batter ready to bake — or you will
have doughy-textured Sourdoughs.

6. Add flour and water the night before
to build up the quantity of Starter
needed — (approximately equal amounts
of flour and water.) This will allow the
Sourdough enzymes to work 10 hours and
remove most of the starch, leaving a
protein food.

7.   Sugar is used as a booster to make the enzymes work faster. It is not used to sweeten the Sourdough.

8. Sugar is used to brown. Too much sugar will make Sourdoughs rubbery.

9. Soda is used to sweeten — reacts against the acid in the <u>Sour</u> dough.

10. Soda is a leavening agent. Add the soda at the very last minute before baking, so the air is in the batter. You will bake fluffy, light Sourdoughs.

11. Lightly cover the Sourdough Pot. Never seal with tight lid as

Sourdough needs to breathe. A piece of foil paper is an excellent cover for the Sourdough Pot.

12. Sourdough may be kept in the refrigerator or cooler when not in constant use. It becomes dormant. Remember to take it out at least a day before using to get the Sourdough enzymes working again. Add flour and water. Keep warm.

Secret for Crisp, Crunchy Sourdoughs: "Stir the soda with the little finger of your left hand, as it is cleaner than the right — and you will eat — 50% Baked Hot AIR!

Food Calls in Alaska

Food's Up !

Soup's On !

Chow Time !

Come and Get it !

What's on the Hook

Coming Up the Next Bucket !

Take it or Leave it !

Eat 'Em Up !

Chow Down !

Let's Eat !

Dinner-r-r-r !